Folens HISTORY Primary

FC0624

CHILDREN LIVING IN VICTORIAN BRITAIN

Mary Green

United Kingdom: Folens Publishers, Apex Business Centre, Boscombe Road, Dunstable, LU5 4RL
Email: folens@folens.com

Ireland: Folens Publishers, Greenhills Road, Tallaght, Dublin 24
Email: info@folens.ie

Poland: JUKA, ul. Renesansowa 38, Warsaw 01-905

Editor: Emma Thomas
Illustrations: Tony Randell

Layout artist: Patricia Hollingsworth
Cover design: Martin Cross

Cover image by permission of Mary Evans Picture Library

First published 2003 by Folens Limited.

British Library Cataloguing in Publication Data. A catalogue record for this publication is available from the British Library.

ISBN 1 84303 062 4

Contents

We hope you enjoy using this new *Primary Specials!* book, to be used with children achieving at a lower level. The book has been written in response to market research with teachers. The focus is a central resource that is entirely visual, with a few exceptions that are written resources, such as historical stories. Accompanying this are support materials. The book follows the revised National Curriculum for History (History 2000) and the QCA scheme of work at Key Stage 2.

New *Primary Specials!* contain 15 separate chapters, each covering a new topic within the theme of the pack. The resource and activity pages are photocopiable and are accompanied by a page of notes for the teacher. This page is laid out as follows:

Background
– gives useful information on the topic, which the teacher can draw on as needed.

Working with the resource
– gives guidance on using the resource as the focus of group discussion, which should be led by the teacher or a support assistant. **Useful questions** are also included.

Using the activity pages
– provides information on the differentiated tasks related to the resource. The activity pages often include graphic organisers such as spidergrams, writing frames and chronological and other models, to support pupils' thinking and recording.

Skills
Important historical skills are included across the books. These should be within the children's abilities, such as:
– promoting the sense of the passage of time
– sequencing events and promoting a sense of chronology
– distinguishing between simple fact and opinion
– recognising that while some things change others stay the same
– promoting empathy through identifying with lives in the past
– recognising simple cause and effect.

Why not look for these other titles in the series?

Ancient Greece	FC0640
Ancient Egypt	FC0616
Children in the Second World War	FC0608
How Life Has Changed Since 1948	FC0632
Invaders and Settlers in Britain	FC0586
Tudor Times	FC0594

Can't find the topic you are looking for? If you have any ideas for other titles to be covered in the *Primary Specials!* series write and let us know:

Publishing Department
Folens Publishers
Unit 20
Apex Business Centre
Boscombe Road
Dunstable
Beds LU5 4RL

Victoria and Albert

Background

Queen Victoria reigned over the country and the British Empire for almost 64 years (1837–1901) and was held up as the wifely ideal and perfect mother. Married to Prince Albert from the age of 18, her marriage was largely successful, but her roles as queen and wife often conflicted. She believed, for example, that a wife should obey her husband and was violently opposed to women's rights, while at the same time believing in her own sovereignty.

Further contradictions are revealed in her letters to the Princess Royal in which she discusses her dislike of child rearing and her belief that unmarried women have greater liberty. She even commented, 'I really think I shall never let your sisters marry … '.

Working with the resource

'Queen Victoria'

This gives a simple account of Victoria's life, highlighting some of the main features and dates. It is best if you read with the children, giving them some opportunity to read aloud themselves. You could refer to the 'Background' section to provide additional information as needed.

Useful questions

1 When did Victoria become queen?
2 Who did she marry?
3 What was the Great Exhibition?
4 How old was her husband when he died?
5 Who was her favourite Prime Minister? What did he help her to do?
6 What was the Diamond Jubilee?
7 How long was Victoria on the throne?

Using the activity sheet

'Victoria's timeline'

All the information the children need to complete the timeline is on this sheet but they must be able to sequence all the dates correctly. (Some children may therefore need to work in pairs.) Once complete the timeline can be kept for reference.

Queen Victoria

Victoria was born in May 1819. When she became queen in 1837 she was only 18 years old. This was the start of the Victorian age.

The young queen could not choose her husband. Her family chose her German cousin. He was called Prince Albert. Victoria and Albert married in 1840 and had a large family.

In 1845 the family moved away from London. They moved to Osborne House on the Isle of Wight. They spent holidays in Scotland at Balmoral Castle.

In the meantime, Albert worked to set up a famous exhibition in London. It was called the Great Exhibition and opened in 1851. Goods and inventions were shown from all over the world.

Queen Victoria

Some years later, in 1861, Albert became very ill with a fever and died. He was only 42 years old. Victoria took Albert's death very badly. She always wore black and would not go out in public for many years.

There were ten Prime Ministers while Victoria was queen. William Gladstone was one, but she did not like him at all. He was too stern for her. She did like another. He was called Benjamin Disraeli. He made her laugh and paid her compliments. He also helped her to appear in public again.

Benjamin Disraeli

William Gladstone

In 1897, when Victoria had been queen for 60 years, there was a celebration. It was called the Diamond Jubilee and everybody had a holiday. Fours years later, in 1901, Victoria died. She had been on the throne longer than any other king or queen.

PRIMARY SPECIALS! *Children in Victorian Britain*

Victoria's timeline

- Write the words and dates in the correct order on the timeline.
- Tick each one as you do it.
- The first has been started for you.

Family moves to Osborne House – 1845   Diamond Jubilee – 1897

Queen Victoria was born – 1819   Albert dies – 1861

Marries Albert – 1840   The Great Exhibition – 1851

Dies – 1901   Becomes queen – 1837

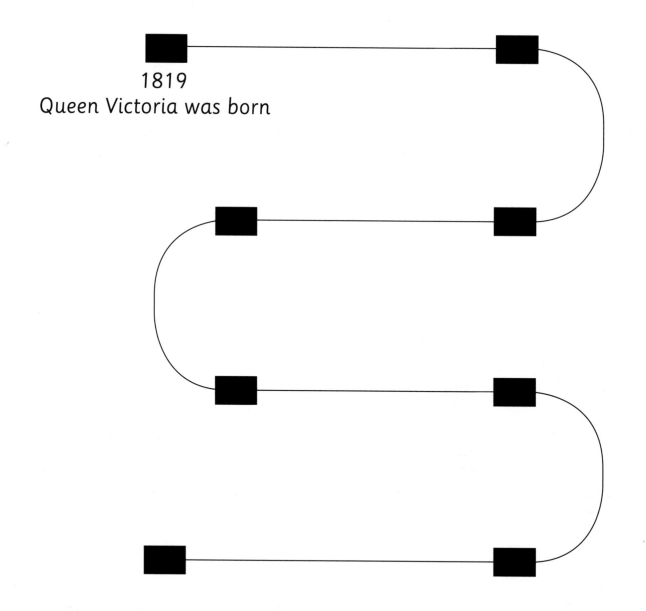

1819
Queen Victoria was born

PRIMARY SPECIALS! *Children in Victorian Britain* © Folens (copiable page)

Wealthy Families

Background

Clara, the central child character in the resource, comes from a *nouveau riche* merchant family of around 1870, often referred to by those further up the social scale as 'in trade'. The wealthy business classes had become increasingly powerful in Victorian society and marriage became a means of improving social status. Clara, as a daughter, would receive an education that would prepare her for a suitable, advantageous marriage.

Women still had few rights at this time. From 1870, a wife had the legal right to keep her own earnings but she could not own property independently as a married woman until 1882. Nor did she have any say over the custody of her children until 1886. Interestingly, by the time Clara has reached adulthood, she would enjoy significantly more rights than her mother did in 1870.

Working with the resource

'Clara's diary'

When discussing the diary, you could explain any unfamiliar terms such as: 'Nanny', 'governess', 'Papa' and 'Mama'. Point to the different relationships Clara has with the other characters. Of these the most important are her close relationship with her nanny; the distance preserved between Clara and her parents; the education Clara receives from her governess. You might also like to compare Clara's life with Harry's. In which case, it may be useful to refer to the unit 'Public Schools' as well.

Useful questions

1 Do you think Clara comes from a rich or poor family? How do you know?
2 Who is Dolly? What does she do?
3 Who is Nanny? Why is she important to Clara?
4 What is a governess? Who is Clara's governess?
5 Who is Harry? What happens to him?

Using the activity sheets

'Clara's spidergram'

There are several relations and members of the household included in Clara's diary that the children should locate and record on the spidergram, along with any jobs they do. The first is given, the remainder are mentioned in order as follows: Fred, the stable boy; Mrs Tibbs, the cook; Dolly, the maid; Nanny, the nurse; Miss James, the governess or teacher; Mr Bell, Harry's tutor or teacher; Harry, Clara's brother; Papa (or Dad); Mama (or Mum); Auntie Edith. Before the children complete the spidergram they could highlight them in the text first.

'A letter to Harry'

The writing frame should help the children to complete the letter. You could encourage them to use information from 'Clara's diary' to flesh out their ideas, particularly the entry for October 9th. Remind the children to use question marks and you could point out that Harry's title would be 'Master'.

Clara's diary

October 4th

We went to church today. Mr Dodds the butler was cross because Fred the stable boy ran off. I like Mrs Tibbs the cook and the maid, Dolly, best. And Nanny, of course. I wore my blue velvet dress and my hair in ringlets. The service was very boring, except when we sang, 'All Things Bright and Beautiful'. Nanny kept telling me to sit up.

October 5th

I have a governess now. Her name is Miss James. She is quite strict. I cannot play much. Nanny says if I'm good and do my lessons Miss James will let me play now and then. Harry's tutor Mr Bell is leaving because Harry is going away to school.

October 6th

I learned chain stitch and cross stitch today. I also learned a new song. Miss James played the piano and we sang it together. She said I have a good voice, if a little squeaky. Tomorrow I will do drawing. Good.

October 7th

I was so sad today. Harry went away to school. He did not want to go. Papa came home from his office. 'Be brave like a man, Harry,' he said. But Harry cried and so did Mama.

October 8th

Aunt Edith brought me a present. Miss James let me play with it when I had learned my four times table. The present is a pack of 20 cards. Whichever way you put them, they make up one long picture!

October 9th

I wrote to Harry. I told him that Miss James is teaching me French now. I asked him if he has made friends. I wonder if Harry is happy.

Clara's spidergram

Who are the people in Clara's diary?
Write them on the spidergram.
Some of them have jobs. What do they do?
Add these to the spidergram by their names.
The first has been done for you.

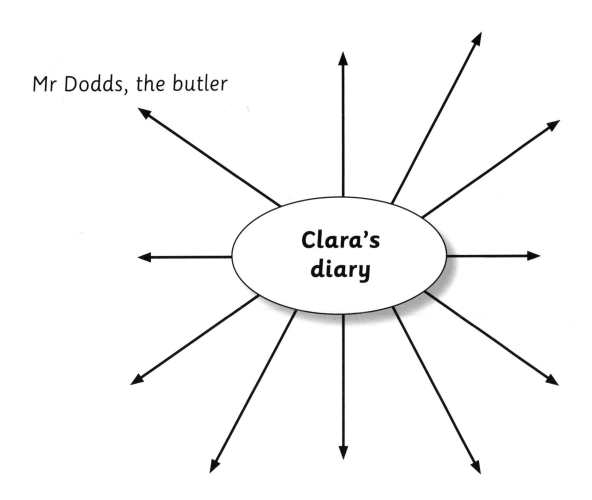

Mr Dodds, the butler

Clara's diary

A letter to Harry

● Read Clara's letter to Harry. Then complete it.

Victoria Villas
Victoria Road
Richly

October 9th

My Dear brother Harry,

How are you? I am well.
I am learning a lot of new things. Miss James

Auntie Edith came to visit. She gave me

How is school, Harry?

What

Who

When

We all miss you very much. Nanny and Mama send their love. Papa sends his kind regards.

Your loving sister,

Clara

PRIMARY SPECIALS! *Children in Victorian Britain*

Domestic Service

Teacher's Notes

This and the units, 'Wealthy Families' and 'Picture Cards and Parlour Games' involve the same fictitious household and you may wish to use them with each other.

Background

The life of a Victorian domestic servant was easier than working in a factory but still required long hours for little pay. The 'below stairs' hierarchy varied according to the establishment. The butler or housekeeper was usually at the top of the pecking order and the scullery maid at the bottom. Where there was only one cook, usually female, she would take orders from or liaise with the housekeeper and be responsible for the household meals for both the family and the servants. Sometimes she would also act as a mother figure to the younger servants. The scullery maid would rarely have been noticed 'upstairs' (perhaps only having contact with the children in the family) and would have been expected to remain unobtrusive as she did her household tasks. Since labour was cheap, even the aspirant middle classes had a maid, though she was likely to live out, coming in on a daily basis. As the century progressed, the working class became increasingly unionised and more powerful. By the end of the First World War, women had tasted some freedom and gained the vote, so domestic servants became less easy to obtain.

Working with the resource

'Below stairs'

The illustration shows the kitchen and the scullery. The former is the cook's, Mrs Tibbs, domain. The latter is where the scullery maid, Dolly, would do much of her work. Apart from preparing meals, the cook would also allot kitchen jobs and train some of the kitchen maids. Discuss the various jobs to be done along with some of the associated vocabulary such as: the 'copper', used for boiling large quantities of water; the 'mangle' for squeezing out water from washing; the wooden slats by the scullery sink, used to prevent slipping over; the 'pantry', used for storing food (and sometimes crockery and cutlery); the kitchen range and dresser, and the 'privy', the toilet.

Useful questions

1 What are the cook's jobs?
2 Can you guess what Dolly's jobs are?
3 Dolly is about your age. How is her life different from yours?
4 How do you think Mrs Tibbs and Dolly get on?

Using the activity sheets

'Kitchen jobs'

The children should match the items listed to their uses. (The less common are explained above.)

'Cook's day'

Here the children have to identify the daily meals and decide what would be eaten under each course at dinner. They could also compare their own meals with those of the family.

Below stairs

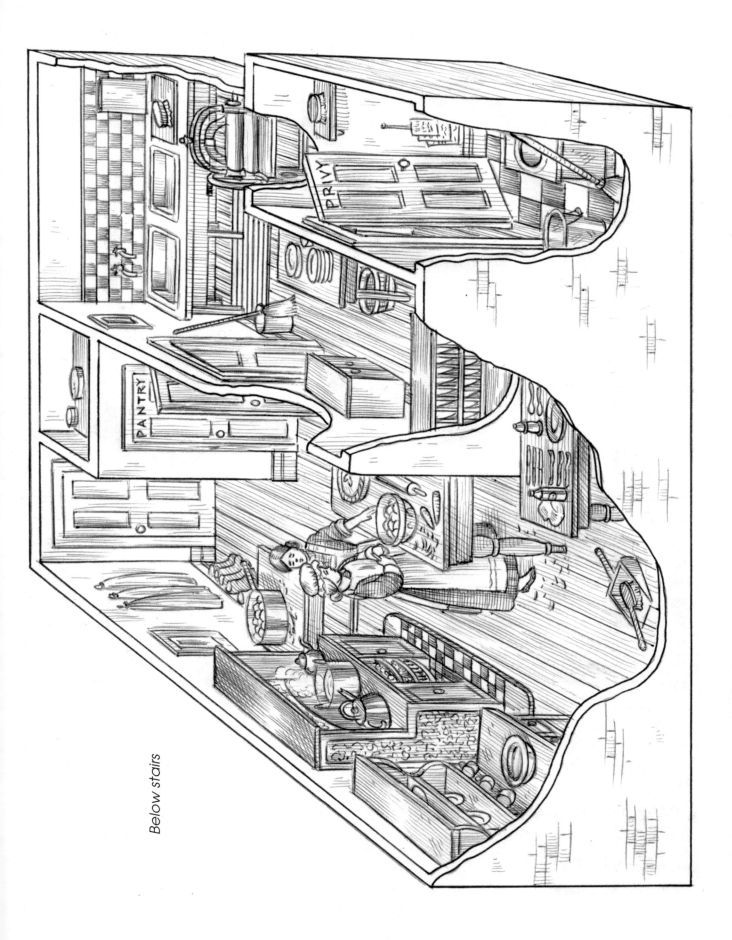

Below stairs

Kitchen jobs

What were these things used for? Can you remember?

● Match the names to their uses like this:

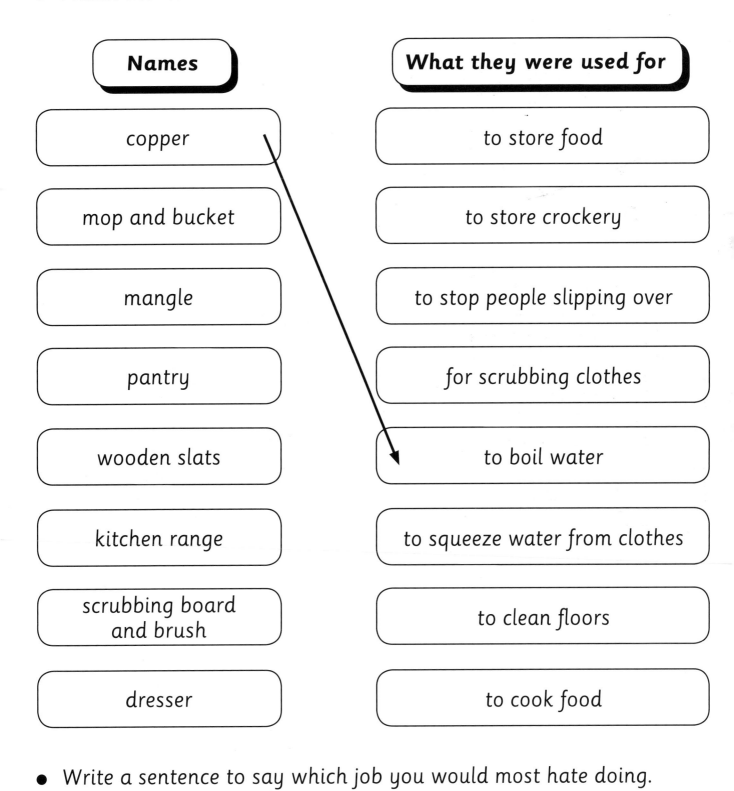

Names	What they were used for
copper	to store food
mop and bucket	to store crockery
mangle	to stop people slipping over
pantry	for scrubbing clothes
wooden slats	to boil water
kitchen range	to squeeze water from clothes
scrubbing board and brush	to clean floors
dresser	to cook food

● Write a sentence to say which job you would most hate doing.

Cook's day

The family had three meals in the daytime. They had breakfast at 9:00am, luncheon at 1:00pm and tea at 4:00pm.

- Write the name and time of each meal under the correct menu.

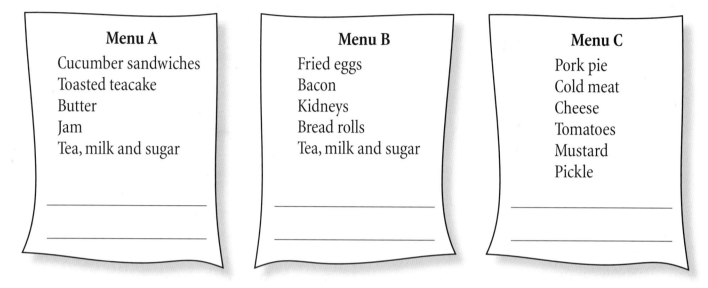

Menu A
Cucumber sandwiches
Toasted teacake
Butter
Jam
Tea, milk and sugar

_____
_____

Menu B
Fried eggs
Bacon
Kidneys
Bread rolls
Tea, milk and sugar

_____
_____

Menu C
Pork pie
Cold meat
Cheese
Tomatoes
Mustard
Pickle

_____
_____

- In the evening they had dinner at 7:30pm. This meal had four courses! Try to guess which course these dishes go under. Then write them in the correct place.

ices   soup   crab   blancmange   duck   lamb   fish
jelly   peas   custard tart   spinach   mint sauce

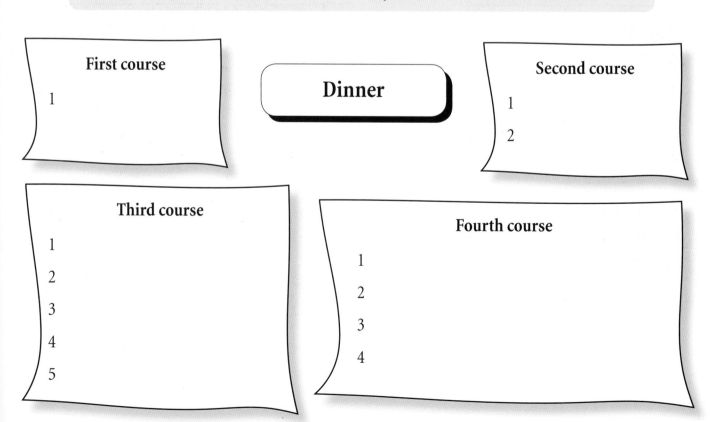

First course
1

Dinner

Second course
1
2

Third course
1
2
3
4
5

Fourth course
1
2
3
4

PRIMARY SPECIALS! *Children in Victorian Britain*

Victorian Street Life

Background

As cities expanded so did the range of occupations. There were thousands of people working on the streets in Victorian times: entertainers, street-crossing sweepers, street sellers, pickpockets and the destitute. There were also numerous small shops such as tailors, haberdashers, tobacconists, pawnbrokers, food shops of various kinds, coaching inns and public houses. For most, life was lived in public. The poor would often assemble in the street or outside their homes. Living in confined spaces such as alleys or tenements meant that being outdoors was often preferable. Women might continue with domestic jobs outside chatting to neighbours as they did so. There were others, often children, who earned their living as scavengers. The mud lark had one of the more bizarre occupations. His life consisted of sifting through mud and waste on the Thames riverbank searching for wood or coal that could be sold on. Even the detritus of a city could amount to a livelihood.

Using the activity sheets

'Sorting them out'

This sheet can be used to classify the different features in the illustration. The children can also refer to it when completing the next activity sheet.

'Our thoughts'

This writing frame can be used to record the group discussion, noting what has changed and what has stayed the same.

Working with the resource

'On the street'

Hidden in the picture are a range of Victorian characters who earned their living on the streets. Ask the children to find them and identify what they do. There is a flower seller, bootlace seller, fire-eater, conjuror, Punch and Judy showman, musician, crossing sweeper, pickpocket, coachman and horse and a beggar woman and her baby. The children might also compare this street with 'Victoria Street' in the unit, 'A Victorian Locality Today'. In addition, they could study illustrations of Victorian genre paintings such as William Powell Frith's *The Railway Station* (1862). There are often stories hidden in them.

Useful questions

1 How many different people can you find in the picture?
2 How many are children?
3 Can you work out what each person is doing?
4 In what way is this street different to our streets?
(Answers might include: the number of children earning their living, the number of trades on the streets, the absence of cars, the use of the horse, the mud and dirt.)
5 In what way is the street the same?
(Answers might include: we still have musicians or buskers, street traders, pickpockets, rough sleepers and some shops would be the same, such as bakeries and fishmongers.)

On the street

Victorian street scene

Sorting them out

- What kinds of things did you see in 'On the street'?
- List them in the correct balloons below.

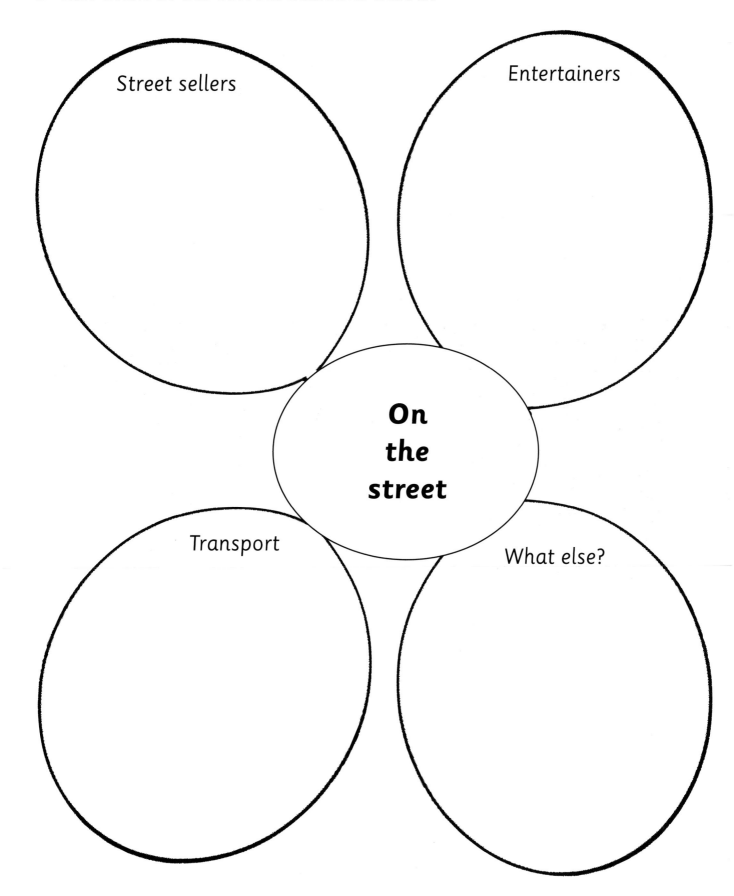

Street sellers

Entertainers

On the street

Transport

What else?

Our thoughts

- Write down what you talked about when you looked at the picture 'On the street'.

I thought that the street was

Someone else said that it was

It was different from streets today. For example,

And

It was also different because

But some things were the same, such as

Mayhew's London

Background

Henry Mayhew's *London Labour and the London Poor* (1851) documents life on the streets of London during the Victorian period. It is probably the most comprehensive account of its kind that still exists and was followed by a similar volume in 1862, focusing on those who made their living illegally. Many of those on the streets were children and Mayhew included several of their stories. The following extract from 'A Watercress Girl' is taken from the first volume. You may like to refer to it in preparation for the resource.

'The poor child, although the weather was severe, was dressed in a thin cotton gown, with a threadbare shawl wrapped round her shoulders ...

"I go about the streets with water-creases, crying 'Four bunches a penny, water-creases.' I am just eight years old ... I gets up in the dark by the light of the lamp in the court. When the snow is on the ground, there's no creases. I bears the cold – you must; so I puts my hand under my shawl, though it hurts them to take hold of the creases, especially when we takes 'em to the pump to wash 'em. No; I never see any child crying – it's no use."'

Working with the resource

'How many pennies?'

The ballad, 'How Many Pennies?' is written in response to Mayhew's account of the watercress girl. The details are accurate. It is best if you read it to the children first. (They might like to join in with the chorus.) You can then discuss the main features.

Useful questions

1 What does the girl sell?
2 How is she dressed?
3 Why do you think she has to work?
4 What do you think these lines mean:

'I may be eight,
But I'm going on twenty'

'Got no time
For sugar sticks'

'If you're born to this,
You've far to go.'

Using the activity sheets

'The watercress girl'

This becomes a character sketch of the watercress girl when the children have recorded their answers in the boxes. The children could work alone and then compare their notes with a partner.

'If you were there ...'

The children should try to think of questions to ask the watercress girl. This should help them empathise with her situation. Useful words are given at the bottom of the page to prompt ideas.

How many pennies?

At four in the morning
I buy my cress,
In threadbare shawl
And cotton dress.

Tie them in bunches
To sell on the street,
Freezing hands,
And freezing feet.

I'm not a child,
I earn my living.
How many pennies
Make a shilling?

Can't go home,
Until they're sold,
These London streets
Aren't paved with gold.

The poor have nothing,
The rich have plenty.
I may be eight,
But I'm going on twenty.

I'm not a child,
I earn my living.
How many pennies
Make a shilling?

Got no time
For sugar sticks,
But I know how many
Pennies make six.

There's sun and rain
There's wind and snow,
If you're born to this,
You've far to go.

I'm not a child,
I earn my living.
How many pennies
Make a shilling?

Mary Green

(Reproduced by kind permission of
Mary Green. © Mary Green, 2003)

PRIMARY SPECIALS! *Children in Victorian Britain*

The watercress girl

● Fill in the boxes about the watercress girl from 'How many pennies?'.

Where is she?

What is she doing?

Why?

What is she wearing?

How old is she?

How does she feel?

Why does she say, 'I'm not a child'?

PRIMARY SPECIALS! *Children in Victorian Britain*

If you were there ...

- If you could meet the watercress girl what questions would you ask her?

Here is an example:

1. What would you wish for most in the world?

2. How

3. Where

4. Have

5. When

6. Who

7. Are

Useful words

home   mother   father   brothers   sisters
food   cruel   money   hungry   streets

- Now ask one more question.

PRIMARY SPECIALS! *Children in Victorian Britain*

The Mill Child

Background

In the first half of the nineteenth century the cotton industry grew rapidly and cities and towns in the North mushroomed. Working conditions, particularly those of women and children, were causing increasing concern among social reformers. Children (as young as six) were cheap to employ and were able to crawl under machinery to clear it of loose cotton. They could also fetch, carry, sweep and clean, and they did this for long periods at a time. Various parliamentary enquiries into child labour were set up and some reforms carried out. Anthony Ashley Cooper (later Lord Shaftesbury) (1801-85) was a notable Victorian social reformer and philanthropist. He was also an MP and a Christian Evangelist who piloted a range of reforms, such as the Coal Mines Act of 1842 and the Factory Act of 1844. The Factory Act required that the hours children aged between eight and thirteen worked could be no more than six and a half a day. This could occur in the morning or afternoon but not both; except for every other day and then for no more than ten hours. Among other things, it also required accidents and deaths to be reported, a register to be kept of the children and young people employed, along with certificates showing that children were attending school.

Working with the resource

'The mill'

Referring to the cotton mill depicted here, explain to the children what child labour was and how children were forced to work long hours in dangerous and unhealthy conditions for little money and often little food. You could point out that some mill owners were cruel and negligent, and beat their child employees. Deaths and serious injuries, such as severed fingers, were also common. The children should also understand that family poverty has always forced children to work (and still does in some parts of the world) and that parents are not necessarily uncaring.

Useful questions

1 What does the mill look like?
2 What are the children doing?
3 Why is it dangerous?
4 Who do you think is in charge?
5 What sort of person is he? Why do you think the children's parents let them work?

Using the activity sheets

'What was it like?'

If the children have studied the picture sufficiently they should be able to identify the correct answers. You will also be alerted to any children who have not grasped some of the main points about mill life.

'What were the results?'

This more challenging sheet deals with cause and effect by the use of the connective 'so'. Some of the statements are closely related and the children need to choose the best match, while rejecting others that may also seem credible. The remaining answers are as follows: 2A, 3G, 4F, 5C, 6B, 7D.

The mill

The mill

PRIMARY SPECIALS! *Children in Victorian Britain*

What was it like?

- Read the following sentences.
- Tick the box beside the sentences that are true.
- Put a cross beside those that are not true.

| | Poor children had to work to earn money. |

| | Rich children worked in mills. |

| | Some children died from working in the mill. |

| | The mill was always kept clean. |

| | Children could be beaten if they did something wrong. |

| | The children did not earn much money. |

| | Only children who were big and strong worked in the mill. |

| | Although the work was hard, the mill was bright and cheerful. |

What were the results?

- Match each line on the left with one on the right. Choose the **best** match.
- Write down your answer like this: **1E**
- Now do the rest in the same way under **Answers**.

1 Some families were poor	**A** so they were very tired.
2 The children had to work long hours	**B** so they were unhealthy places.
3 The children had little food	**C** so mill owners used children as workers.
4 The children crawled under machines	**D** so they tried to change the law.
5 Children were paid less than adults	**E** so children had to earn money.
6 There was little fresh air in the mills	**F** so they often got hurt.
7 Some people cared about the children	**G** so they were often hungry.

Answers

1E

The Ragged School Movement

Background

The first ragged school (1818) began before Victoria came to the throne but the idea had considerable impact during her reign. It is credited to John Pounds (1766–1839), a Portsmouth shoemaker. The story goes that while working in his shop he saw many waifs on the street and began to teach one or two of them to read, do simple arithmetic and learn practical skills. Increasing numbers of children attended and soon a little school had begun, free of charge. The idea of charitable education for street children was taken up by various philanthropists, including the Reverend Thomas Guthrie. With his support, further schools were developed in Scotland during the 1840s. Lord Shaftesbury founded the Ragged Schools' Union in 1844, which further promoted the institution in England and by the 1870s hundreds of thousands of children had passed through the system.

Using the activity sheets

'John Pounds'

In the first part of the activity, the children are asked to distinguish between fact and opinion. Then they are asked to add an opinion of their own, backing it up with some simple evidence about John Pounds.

'School'

The writing frame should help the children to compare their own experience of school with John Pounds' school. They need to make the final point from the perspective of a nineteenth century child and consider whether being on the streets was preferable to going to school.

Working with the resource

'The ragged school'

The illustration gives an impression of what John Pounds' school would have been like. (Later ragged schools would have been more formal and a wider range of subjects taught.) Encourage the group to deduce that teaching the children would not have been easy since they were used to an unrestricted, albeit hard, life on the streets. Many would have been beyond control but not all and, since John Pounds' school became popular, we can assume that most children would have benefited in some way from attending. You can also point out that a simple idea, if taken up, can have a lasting historical effect.

Useful questions

1 What is the room like?
2 Can you find the teacher?
3 What is he doing?
4 What other job do you think he does?
5 What are the children doing?
6 What do you think they are learning?
7 How is it different from your school?

The ragged school

The ragged school

PRIMARY SPECIALS! *Children in Victorian Britain* © Folens (copiable page)

John Pounds

- Read the sentences about John Pounds. They are either a fact (true) or an opinion (someone's point of view).

- Tick the correct box for each sentence.

	Fact	Opinion
John Pounds was born in 1766.	☐	☐
He began to teach children in 1818.	☐	☐
He had too many children to teach.	☐	☐
He taught children to read.	☐	☐
John Pounds should have made the children sit still.	☐	☐
In my view, John Pounds was a very kind man.	☐	☐
John Pounds was a shoemaker.	☐	☐
I think he was tired of making shoes so he became a teacher.	☐	☐
John Pounds died in 1839.	☐	☐

- Write down an opinion of your own about John Pounds.

I think John Pounds was

because

School

- How is your school different from John Pounds' school?

In my school the room

Our chairs and tables

And also

But in John Pounds' school there are

This is because

Some things we learn are the same, such as

But we do not learn

If I were a child at John Pounds' school, I would have liked /not liked school because

Public Schools

Teacher's Notes

This unit refers back to 'Wealthy Victorian Families'. The children may have completed the 'Letter to Harry' sheet, but if not, it can be done in conjunction with the activity sheet below, 'Harry replies to Clara'.

Background

Despite its prestige, the nineteenth century public school curriculum was limited. (The confusing term 'public' for what is a fee-paying school originates in the sixteenth century and refers to what was then a grammar school maintained from the public purse.) The classics, sport and mathematics were emphasised. The primary object was to produce a 'gentleman'; a man of 'character' who was capable of maintaining his position in society and whose values included patriotism, loyalty to one's class and tradition. To this end, life at school was often brutal. There were strict hierarchies among the pupils and considerable bullying. *Tom Brown's Schooldays* by Thomas Hughes, published in 1856, gives an accurate picture of nineteenth-century boarding-school life.

Working with the resource

'Going away to school'

You may need to remind the children that the sons of the wealthy were sent away to school. Explain that boys who were good at sport were believed to be strong and tough; qualities they believed made good leaders. You could also point out that a great deal of bullying went on and that older boys treated younger boys like servants. This touching letter will give the children some idea of the experiences undergone by most public-school boys.

Useful questions

1 What has happened to Freddy?

2 What do you think his father will do? (Think carefully!)

3 Do you know any stories about boarding school? What are they like? (Children are likely to be aware of the Harry Potter books.)

4 How is your school different? Is it similar in any way?

Using the activity sheets

'Freddy'

The children are asked to record how Freddy feels about his situation. They can draw on the their previous discussion of his letter.

'Harry replies to Clara'

The writing frame suggests that Harry is having a mixed experience at public school, but is saved from complete misery by his sporting skills. The children can call on the activity sheet 'Freddy' for further information.

Going away to school

My dear dear Mother,

If you don't let me come home I die – I am all over ink,
and my fine clothes have been spoilt – I have been tost
in a blanket, and seen a ghost.

I remain, my dear dear Mother,
Your dutiful and most unhappy son,
Freddy.

P.S. Remember me to my Father.

From *Westminster School* by J. D. Carleton

PRIMARY SPECIALS! *Children in Victorian Britain*   © Folens (copiable page)

Freddy

● Answer the questions in the boxes.

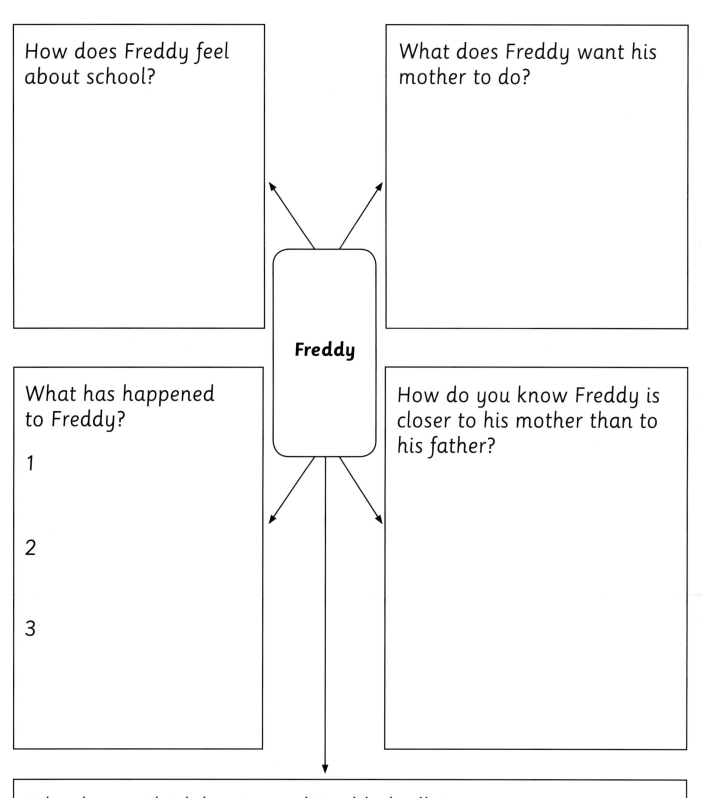

How does Freddy feel about school?	What does Freddy want his mother to do?

Freddy

What has happened to Freddy? 1 2 3	How do you know Freddy is closer to his mother than to his father?

Who do you think has treated Freddy badly?

Harry replies to Clara

Can you remember that Harry, Clara's brother, went away to school? Clara sent him a letter.

● Finish Harry's reply.

The Meadows School
Pipham
Wessex

October 10th

My Dearest Clara,
Thank you for your letter.
The first night here was very bad. The other boys

They

I was

But as you know Clara, I am good at sport. So now the boys

I still miss home and

I hope to see you soon.
Your loving brother,

Harry

P.S.

PRIMARY SPECIALS! *Children in Victorian Britain* © Folens (copiable page)

Compulsory Education

Background

The Education Act of 1870 marked the departure from voluntary education to a compulsory, elementary one and came about partly as a result of working class agitation over many years, culminating in the vote for male householders in 1867. The Board School (so called because it came under the management of a school board) was established. Prior to that, education had been voluntary. Provision for the poor and working class had been a haphazard affair of ragged schools, factory schools, dame schools (usually run by elderly women), church schools and others. The wealthy had attended public school and the middle classes the grammar school. However, even after 1870, the different classes continued to receive different levels of education. This was also true of the sexes. In the 1870s, for example, girls spent a great proportion of the week doing needlework or housewifery of one sort or another. There were some notable exceptions. The North London Collegiate, established by Frances Mary Buss (1827–94), provided a wide curriculum for girls. She and her friend Dorothea Beale were also campaigners for higher education for women.

Working with the resource

'The Victorian classroom'

The illustration clearly shows that girls and boys were educated separately and that order and regimentation was emphasised (though by no means always achieved). Victorian buildings of this type still exist, though modernised and extended. Your school may be one of them, in which case the children can compare this example with their own school as it might once have been.

Useful questions

1 Who is in the class? How is this different from most schools today?

2 What are the children doing? How are they seated?

3 What things are on the teacher's desk? What are these used for?

4 How is the school different in other ways from a modern school?

Using the activity sheets

'What did the children learn?'

The children could work in pairs to discuss and complete the tasks. They should be able to identify the important curriculum differences, though they might not realise that only boys did science, if it was taught at all. They can also compare their own curriculum with that of Victorian children. (Please note some poorer schools only offered the 3Rs, scripture, geography, and sewing and knitting for the girls.) The answers are as follows: both did reading, writing, arithmetic, RE, PE, history and geography. The boys did woodwork and science. The girls did sewing, washing clothes, housekeeping and knitting.

'The logbook'

Schools were expected to keep logbooks, which the inspector would read. Entries often recorded absences, school closure and behaviour, along with more pleasant events such as celebrations. The entries on the activity page, though fictitious, typify the kind of entries that would have been made, but are simpler so the children can use them as models. The ideas at the bottom of the page should also help children complete the task.

The Victorian classroom

The Victorian classroom

PRIMARY SPECIALS! *Children in Victorian Britain*

What did the children learn?

Boys and girls did not always do the same lessons in Victorian schools.

● Who do you think did these lessons? Tick the boxes to say.
Tick one box only for each lesson.

	Boys	Girls	Both
Reading			
Sewing			
Washing clothes (laundry)			
Writing			
Arithmetic			
Woodwork			
PE			
Science			
RE (scripture)			
History			
Housekeeping			
Knitting			
Geography			

The logbook

Victorian teachers wrote comments about school life in a book.
It was called a logbook.

● Read these entries.

> December 19th
>
> Snow very thick on the ground today. Not one child arrived. School closed.

> April 3rd
>
> Vera T. threw her slate at Jean M. Sent Vera home, but she would not go. Stayed outside all afternoon.

● Now write three more entries. Choose from the words below to give you ideas.

June 7th

September 4th

November 22nd

Useful words

flu   haymaking   birthday   wind and rain   market   inspector

Education and Welfare

Background

Poor attendance was a major problem in many Victorian board schools. But conditions did not encourage attendance. Apart from illness and the necessity of keeping children away from school to work, many country children had to walk long distances to school in all weathers. Furthermore, the welfare of children was not seen by many school boards as part of their role. There was frequently no adequate heating, no opportunity to change wet clothes and any food eaten would have to be brought from home. There was also a fee of a few pence per week, which was not abolished until 1891. Despite the Education Act of 1870 some schools had no proper buildings and were still run by families who would leave older pupils (pupil-teachers) in charge. Although the cane and birch were used and regimes could be very harsh, there were also kindly teachers who knew families well and in the absence of any organised welfare, would provide boots and clothes for the poorer children.

Working with the resource

'A very wet day'

The children can read this short scene together. It encourages them to empathise with the trials and tribulations of the country-school child. They can speculate about what might happen next and you may wish to add further information about Victorian village life. For example, the children are likely to be known in a close-knit community, and relatives or trusted adults would live near by. You may wish to explain the words and expressions, 'wailing fit to bust', 'ain't' and 'mutt' before beginning.

Useful questions

1 Why are the children in a mess?
2 What happens to them when they get to school?
3 Who is Joan?
4 What will happen to the children if they go home?
5 What do you think they will do now?

Using the activity sheet

'The next scene'

The children are asked to explore ideas and anticipate what might happen to the characters next. Some help is given to start them off. They can then choose a scene to improvise in a small group in which the situation is resolved or made worse.

A very wet day

It is almost 8:00am. May, Jack and Daisy live in a small cottage. They have a long walk to school.

Jack: Why do we have to go again? It's the end of the week.

Mother: May, don't forget the school money. It's on the table.
May picks it up.

Jack: But do we have to go, mother?

Mother: Be quiet Jack. You must go and that's that. Here, take your father's scarf and mine too, for Daisy.

May: But our boots, mother. Jack's ain't dry. Daisy's is shrunk. And mine are full a holes.

Mother: And mind you look after Daisy and Jack, May. *She pushes them out the door.*
Go on now!

The children trudge up a dirt track. It starts to rain. Their dog Thunder follows.

Jack: Here, boy!

May: Home, Thunder, home! You ain't coming today. And get out of that mud, Jack!

Two miles later. They are all tired.

Jack: How much longer? Can't we stop, May?

Daisy: My feet are all sore May; I can't walk. *She starts to cry.*

May: Jack, give Daisy a piggyback will you?

A very wet day (continued)

It is 9:00am. The children arrive at the village school. They are in an awful state. An older girl, Joan, who helps the teacher, is standing at the door.

Joan: Well, May Baker, you 'aint coming in here lookin' like that.

May: But … we're soaking wet and Daisy's wailing fit to bust.

Joan: Your Jack's like a mud pie. And he shouldn't be here. He has to go in the boy's entrance.

Thunder runs forward barking.

Joan: And you can't bring that mutt in here. This is a school! *She kicks out.*
Get back you brute!

Joan bangs the door shut. The children are left outside in the rain.

Mary Green

The next scene

- What do you think May, Jack and Daisy do next?

- Here is the start of five more ideas. Finish them and write them in the box.

---

1 The children begin their walk home, but

2 Joan is told off by the teacher and sent out to

3 The children's Gran lives

4 Thunder the dog

5 May decides they will spend

- Choose one idea and act the next scene.

A Victorian Locality Today

Teacher's Notes

Teacher's Notes
You might like to use the resource 'Victoria Street' below for comparison with the unit, 'Victorian Street Life'.

Background

Periods of great economic growth are often reflected in the grandeur of their buildings. The Victorians left behind numerous examples of civic pride such as town halls and government buildings that were often Gothic in style. This Gothic revival recalled the architecture of the medieval cathedral and is evident in such buildings as the Houses of Parliament, built by Barry and Pugin between 1840 and 1860 and St Pancras Station (1868). In the middle-class Victorian villa, domestic architecture also reflected this style. However, these were largely built in the expanding suburbs, where the middle class went to escape the grime and poverty of the city streets. Once alerted, the children should be able to recognise the numerous examples of Victorian architecture in their locality; the typical red-brick villa, church or school with its deep roof, gables and decorative arches.

Using the activity sheets

'Looking closely'

The children can use the activity sheet to record information about the illustration. This should encourage them to observe details in preparation for simple fieldwork.

'Fact file'

This can be used if the children are taken out on a field trip or visit. It should help them to focus on a single feature, such as a Victorian window. (They will in effect be studying source material.) They should try to draw the example as accurately as they can, observing shape and decoration. They can then make notes in the fact file.

Working with the resource

'Victoria Street'

This kind of street scene can be found in many towns and the illustration can be used before fieldwork to reinforce typical features of Victorian architecture. The differences between these buildings and the modern office block and garage can be discussed. You might also like to refer to the other modern features in the picture, such as the cars, pointing out that these would not have existed during the Victorian period.

Useful questions

1 What buildings are in this picture? What are they used for?
2 Have you seen buildings like this before? Where?
3 Which are Victorian? Which are modern?
4 How are they different?
5 What materials have been used to build them? (e.g. Victorian buildings: brick, slate; Modern buildings: concrete, glass.)

Victoria Street

Victoria Street

Looking closely

● Write down what you can see in the picture of the street.

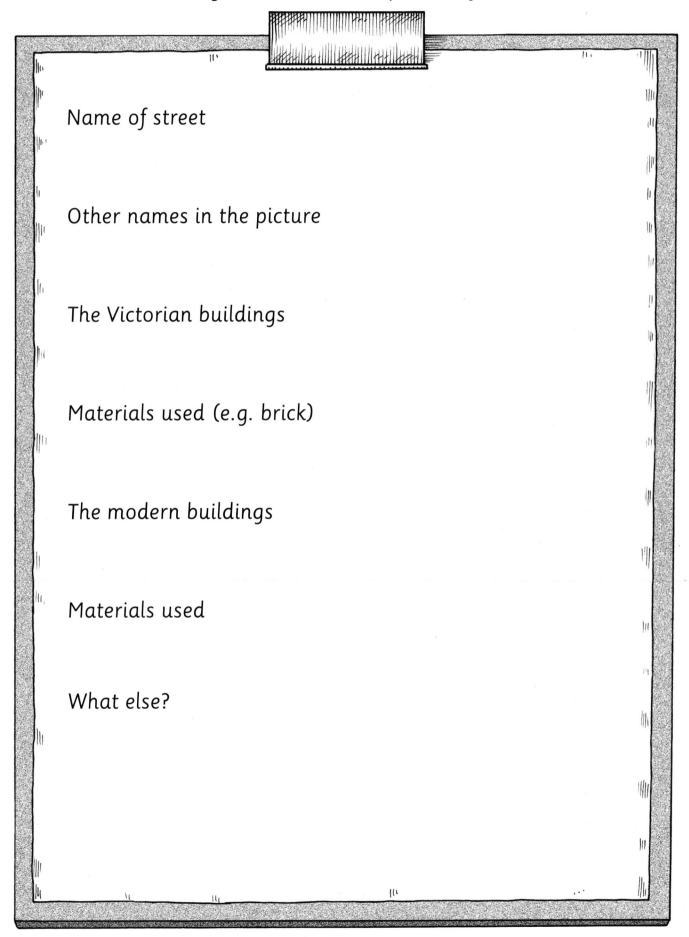

Name of street

Other names in the picture

The Victorian buildings

Materials used (e.g. brick)

The modern buildings

Materials used

What else?

Fact file

1 Choose one part of a Victorian building to draw. It could be the window, porch or roof.

Draw your picture here. Draw all the details.

2 Now fill in the fact file.

Fact file

What is it? ● _____

What is it made of? ● _____

What kind of building does it belong to? ● _____

Where is the building? ● _____

Write down the date of the building, if you know it. ● _____

What else? ● _____

PRIMARY SPECIALS! *Children in Victorian Britain* © Folens (copiable page)

Crafts and Decoration

Background

Between the1840s and 1870s the typical middle-class Victorian parlour would be decorated with wallpaper (sometimes flocked), velvet or leather upholstery, tasselled curtains and eastern rugs. Rooms were heavily furnished and there were many paintings, tapestries and ornaments. Conspicuous wealth was a mark of success. The Victorian house would also display a range of features including stucco (plaster decorations or coating), tiled floor patterns and etched or stained glass. The last of these had increased in popularity throughout the period and exceptional examples could be found (and still can) in churches, colleges and other institutions. Earlier in the nineteenth century stained glass tended to consist of different coloured glass separated by lead but later it also incorporated painting with borders or repeating motifs. The Arts and Crafts Movement, which involved William Morris, Edward Burne-Jones, Dante Gabriel Rossetti and others, included stained glass among their many interests. Burne-Jones was one of the greatest stained-glass designers of the period.

Useful questions

1 What colours did you experiment with?

2 What colours did you choose? Why?

3 How did you make your stained-glass window?

4 How is your stained glass similar to real stained glass? (Point to the effect of the light passing through the paper.)

Working with the resources

'Make a stained-glass window'

If necessary discuss with the children what stained glass is, pointing out that a brilliant colour is created when the light passes through it. The two resource pages will allow the children to produce a mock stained-glass window and can be used as follow-up work after a field trip or visit. They will need scissors, glue and coloured tissue paper or other suitable materials such as transparent sweet wrappers or plastic. Laying one piece of tissue paper over another can also make a new colour. (For example, red and blue to make purple.) Go through the resources with the children ensuring they understand the instructions, which are as follows:

'Make a stained-glass window: the frame'

1 Cut around the outer dotted line to make a window frame.

2 Cut around the inside dotted line to begin your window.

'Make a stained-glass window: the cut-out'

1 and 2 Cut and fold the window in half.

3 Cut out patterns.

4 and 5 Open out and stick different coloured tissue paper behind patterns.

6 Paste to window frame.

Encourage the children to experiment with colours before they make their final choices. Please note that the instructions are also given on the sheets.

Using the activity sheet

'My window'

The children can use this frame to make an assessment of their work.

Make a stained-glass window: the frame

1 Cut around the outer dotted line to make a window frame.

2 Cut around the inside dotted line to begin your window.

PRIMARY SPECIALS! *Children in Victorian Britain*

Make a stained-glass window: the cut-out

1 Cut out **A**.

A

2 Fold it in half like this:

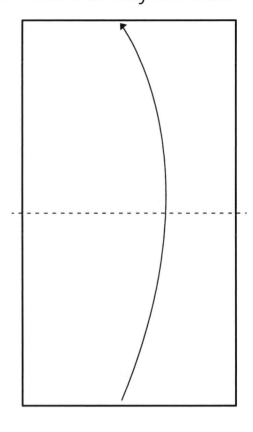

4 Open it like this:

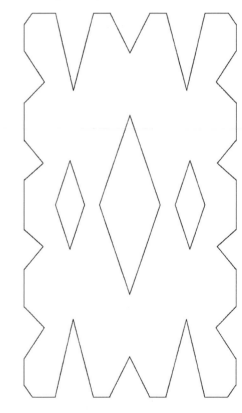

3 Cut out patterns like this:

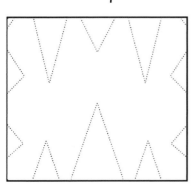

5 Stick coloured tissue paper behind the cut-out.

6 Paste the cut-out to the window frame.

My window

- Write about your stained-glass window.

To make my stained-glass window I used

I was pleased with

The pattern is like

The window is not the same as real stained glass because

But in one way it is, because

Useful words

tissue paper   scissors   glue   design   light   shines   colour

Picture Cards and Parlour Games

Teacher's Notes

This and the units, 'Wealthy Families' and 'Domestic Service' involve the same fictitious household and you may wish to use them with each other.

Background

Present-day children might consider how different life would be without television, computers and the cinema for entertainment. Victorian families enjoyed musical evenings, cards and tableaux as well as visits to the theatre, music halls and pantomime at Christmas. They also enjoyed parlour games such as 'Hunt the Thimble' and 'Blind Man's Buff' (in which the blindfolded person must identify whoever they collide with). There was, too, great interest in card tricks, illusion and optical toys such as the kaleidoscope and the Magic Lantern show – an early method of projecting images onto a screen. In Clara's diary, in the unit 'Wealthy Families', Aunt Edith gives Clara a series of 20 or more cards that could be laid out in any order to make a continuous picture. This popular novelty was called a Myriorama, examples of which can be found in the Bethnal Green Museum of Childhood, London.

Working with the resource

'The never-ending picture'

These eight cards should give the children an impression of what a Myriorama was like. The secret of its success lies in the continuous horizontal lines of the landscape, which match across all cards. You could ask the children to cut out the pictures or do it yourself and discuss how the Myriorama works. You may need to explain the term 'horizon'.

Instructions

Cut out the cards, making sure they fit together perfectly (i.e. no blank spaces between each card).

Useful questions

1 What happens when you lay the cards out one after the other?
2 What happens if you change the cards around? (Try it several different ways.)
3 Can you work out why there is always a complete picture?

Using the activity sheet

'Make your own never-ending picture'

The examples on the page give the children a head start in creating their own Myriorama because the line of the horizon is in place. They can, of course, add as many pictures as they like. However, they will need to remember what they have learned and maintain the line of the horizon across all the cards.

The never-ending picture

The never-ending picture

The never-ending picture (continued)

The never-ending picture

Make your own never-ending picture

- Finish the first three pictures.
- Then draw the fourth on your own.

Remember to keep the line of the horizon so that the pictures join.

PRIMARY SPECIALS! *Children in Victorian Britain*

The Punch and Judy Show

Background

The character of Punch dates back to at least sixteenth-century Italy and was originally an ill-mannered buffoon (Pulcinella) in the perfomances of the *Commedia Dell'Arte*. These were travelling Italian theatrical troupes. The character reached his heyday in Britain during the nineteenth century in the Punch and Judy show. All classes watched performances, either in their drawing rooms or on the streets. Payne Collier published the first transcript of a Punch and Judy Show *The Tragical Comedy, or Comical Tragedy, of Punch and Judy* with George Cruikshank, Dickens' illustrator, providing the pictures. Henry Mayhew also recorded the performance of a Punch and Judy street performer along with the script in *London Labour and the London Poor* (1851).

As working hours became regulated and bank holidays were introduced so visits to the seaside increased, where the Punch and Judy show was a beach entertainment. Characters and stories vary hugely but a typical plot involves Mr Punch throwing the baby away after hitting it with his slapstick (from which the term 'slapstick comedy' comes) attacking Judy and most other characters, being arrested and sentenced by the beadle (judge) and persuading the hangman to change places with him. The only creature he finds daunting is the crocodile who, along with everyone else, loves sausages.

Working with the resource

'Punch and Judy'

Give the children some information about a Punch and Judy show and recount the plot. Some of the children might have watched a performance, in which case they could contribute. Also discuss why the character of Punch has lasted for so long. (Perhaps, because the villain is always more interesting.) You may wish to discuss Punch's violence and the children could consider whether or not the content of some television cartoons are as violent.

Useful questions

1 What kinds of things might happen in a Punch and Judy show?
2 What do you think the slapstick was for?
3 Mr Punch often wins in the end. Why do you think this is?
4 Why do you think the booth was so tall?
5 Have you ever heard the term, 'pleased as Punch'? Can you guess where it comes from and what it means?

Using the activity sheets

'Mr Punch'

Using what they have learned the children can record information about Mr Punch and build up a character sketch. You could also adapt the activity sheet to suit other characters.

'Roll up! Roll up!'

Once the children have finished their adverts they could add further decoration, such as pictures of Punch and the other characters.

Punch and Judy

Punch and Judy

 PRIMARY SPECIALS! *Children in Victorian Britain*

Mr Punch

● Fill in the boxes about Mr Punch.

His family

Bad points

Who he is afraid of

Any good points?

What the law does

What happens to him at the end?

Roll up! Roll up!

● Make up an advert for a Punch and Judy Show.
It has been started for you.

Roll up! Roll up!

For

To take place on

Watch

See

And laugh at

All shows at the following times

Useful names

Mr Punch   Judy   The Baby   Toby (the dog)   The Policeman
The Judge   Joey the Clown   The Hangman   The Crocodile

Useful words

beach pier puppets slapstick sausages 11:00am 2:00pm 4:00pm

A Victorian Christmas Card

Background

Victorian Christmas cards became popular in the 1870s. They were often highly decorative, depicting Christmas scenes. Some were cut-outs, some pop-ups, while others, like the one on the activity sheet, folded open, to display an alternative scene. The picture chosen is of a Victorian villa, which opens out to display the hearth at Christmas.

Using the activity sheet

'Inside the house'

Once the children have completed their cards they could use them to explore who might live in the house and what kind of celebrations are going on. In answer to the questions on the activity sheet, they can either draw more pictures to create a storyboard or discuss ideas with a partner. Victorian names are given at the bottom of the page to help the children.

You might also like to use the cards in conjunction with a story, for example 'The Little Match Girl' by Hans Christian Andersen (1805–75) from *Hans Andersen's Fairy Tales* (Oxford University Press 1984). The beggar-child in the story imagines herself inside a warm domestic scene on Christmas Eve, a scene similar to the ones the children will have made for their cards. You could also refer back to the watercress girl and the children could imagine her response in a similar situation.

Working with the resource

'A Victorian Christmas card'

Making this Christmas card is not difficult and makes an effective display. The cut-outs can be stuck on by the children and coloured in, or if they prefer, they can add their own pictures. They could also add glitter, cotton wool or any other suitable material. Ask them to write an appropriate greeting. Many families send and receive Christmas cards in the UK, regardless of their religion. However, those who do not celebrate Christmas could create their own card for a similar occasion. Cards are often sent at Diwali for instance.

Instructions

You can demonstrate how to make the card, or if you prefer the following instructions can be given to the children:

1 Cut out the card.
2 Fold the flaps over.
3 Draw windows and a door on the front.
4 Cut out the pictures on the second sheet.
5 Stick them on the inside of the card.
6 Colour the card.
7 Write a greeting on the back and sign your name.

A Victorian Christmas card

● Make a Victorian
  Christmas card.

A Victorian Christmas card

A Victorian Christmas card

Inside the house

Who lives in the house?	
What decorations are there?	
What is happening? Why?	
Why are they celebrating?	
When are they celebrating?	

Here are some names that were popular in Victorian times for you to choose from:

Alice   Amy   Amelia   Emily   Laura   Lucy   Victoria

Albert   Alfred   Charles   Conrad   Edward   Edwin   Henry